A BATH A...

THE PEDI...

1 BATH
2 SALISBURY
3 WELLS
4 OXFORD

More titles to follow; for a full list and for a catalogue of all our titles please contact:

Ex Libris Press
1 The Shambles
Bradford on Avon
Wiltshire, BA15 1JS
Tel/Fax 01225 863595

Cover: Queen Street;
Overleaf: View across the King's Bath to Bath Abbey

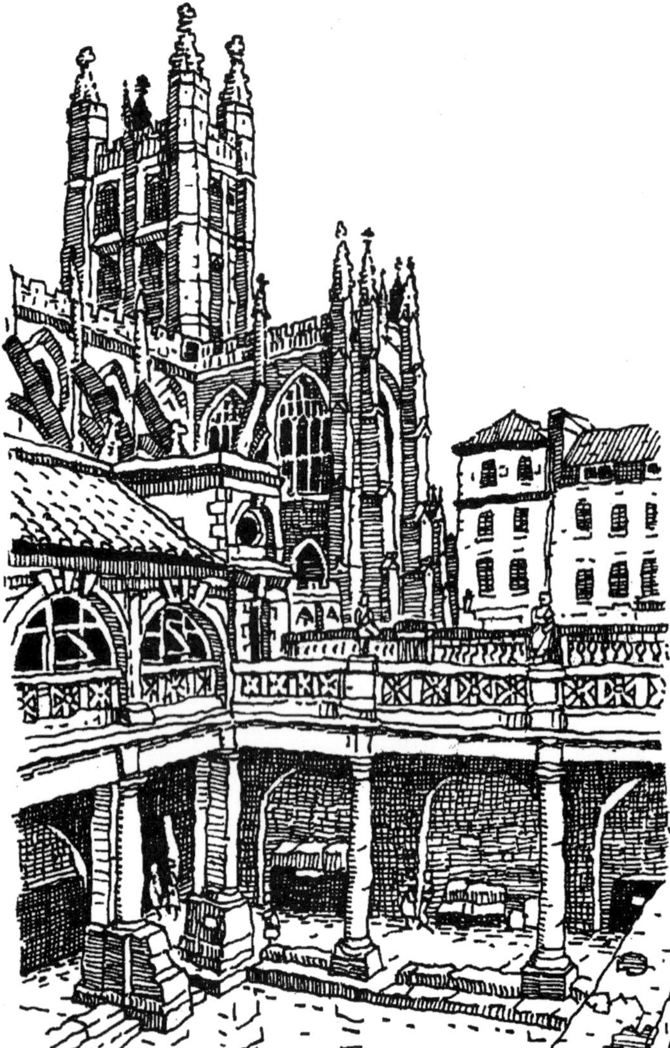

PEDLAR'S PACK 1

A BATH ASSORTMENT

collected and presented
by
JOHN CHANDLER

Illustrations by Simon Gane

EX LIBRIS PRESS

Published in 1996 by
EX LIBRIS PRESS
1 The Shambles
Bradford on Avon
Wiltshire
BA15 1JS

Design and typesetting by
Ex Libris Press

Cover printed by Shires Press, Trowbridge
Printed and bound by Cromwell Press, Melksham

© John Chandler (text) 1996
© Simon Gane (illustrations) 1996

ISBN 0 948578 79 3

Contents ~

Bath in a Nutshell	6
A BATH ASSORTMENT	9
Sources and Acknowledgements	77
A Miscellany of Explanations	79
Index	80

Bath in a Nutshell ~

This book is an anthology, a collection of some of the cleverest, wittiest, and most evocative writing about Bath, in poetry and prose, from Roman times to the twentieth century. Perhaps you are already very familiar with the history of Bath. If so, you will recognize the characters and places which turn up in the following pages. If not, here stripped to essentials, is what you need to remember:

☞   Bath owes its name, and much of its importance throughout history, to the hot mineral water springs around which it is built.

☞   The Romans, attracted by these springs, built baths and temples here, and established a city which they called Aquae Sulis, 'the waters of Sulis'. Sulis was the Celtic goddess of the springs, which the Romans identified with their goddess Minerva.

☞   After Roman rule ended, the town decayed, but its walls remained. A Saxon town and abbey were established within them, and Bath continued throughout the middle ages as a small but important market and clothmaking town.

☞   The curative effects of bathing in the miraculous waters were recognized during the middle ages and later, but it was not until a few years before 1700 that Bath began to be a fashionable resort. People began drinking the water, as well as bathing in it.

☞   The eighteenth century was Bath's heyday. Anyone with money and social pretensions came here, and a leisure industry based on fashion, etiquette, and matchmaking developed. The city expanded rapidly to cater for the visitors, and splendid terraces, crescents and squares were built of the local stone.

☞   As well as coming to Bath for the season, leisured people began to settle here, especially in old age. The city, by 1800 the ninth largest in England, became a fashionable place for retirement.

☞   Genteel, elegant and cultured, Bath has continued also as an important centre of commerce and industry. Gradually its Roman past has been uncovered, and it is now on every tourist's itinerary. The Roman baths, the medieval abbey, and the unsurpassed Georgian and Regency architecture are famous throughout the world.

All of this you will find elaborated in the following pages. At the end there is a short miscellany of explanations of some of the more obscure references which may trip you up, and a brief index.

John Chandler
East Knoyle, April 1996

Quiet Street

Can you remember your first impression of Bath? Was it as a sightseer, soaking up the architecture, the crowds, the steamy atmosphere of the baths themselves? Imagine, then, the excitement of a first visit when Georgian Bath was in full swing, seen here through the eyes of a fictional servant girl, Smollett's Winifred Jenkins.

DEAR GIRL, I have seen all the fine shews of Bath; the Prades, the Squires and the Circlis, the Crashit, the Hottogon, and Bloody Buildings, and Harry King's row; and I have been twice in the Bath with mistress, and n'ar a smoak upon our backs hussy – The first time I was mortally afraid, and flustered all day; and afterwards made believe that I had got the heddick; but mistress said, if I didn't go I should take a dose of bumtaffy; and so remembering how it worked Mrs Gwyllim a pennorth, I chose rather to go again with her into the Bath, and then I met with an axident. I dropt my petticoat, and could not get it up from the bottom. – But what did that signify; they mought laff, but they could see nothing; for I was up to the sin in water. To be sure, it threw me into such a gumbustion, that I know not what I said, nor what I did, nor how they got me out, and rapt me in a blanket – Mrs Tabitha scoulded a little when we got home; but she knows as I know what's what.

A Bath Assortment

First-time visitors usually head for the baths, and the abbey. This is how it has always been.

WE CAME before night to the Bath. Where I presently stepped out with my landlord and saw the baths with people in them. They are not so large as I expected but yet pleasant and the town most of stone and clean though the streets generally narrow.

Strange to see how hot the water is and in some places though this is the most temperate bath the springs so hot as the feet not to endure. But strange to see what women and men herein that live all the season in these waters that cannot but be parboiled and look like the creatures of the Bath.

Up and walked up and down the town and saw a pretty good market place and many good street and fair stone houses and so to the great church and there saw Bp Montagu's tomb and when placed did there see many brave people come and among other two men brought in litters and set down in the chancel to hear. But I did not know one face. Here a good organ but a vain pragmatic fellow preached a ridiculous sermon affected that made me angry and some gent. that sat next me and sang well. So home walking round the walls of the city which are good and the battlem'ts all whole. So home to dinner, and after dinner comes Mr Butts again to see me and he and I to church where the same idle fellow preached. And I slept most of the sermon. Thence home and took my wife out and the girls and came to this church again to see it and look over the monuments where among others Dr Venner and Pelling and a lady of Sir W. Waller's he lying with his face broken. So to the fields a little and walked and then home and had my head looked and so to supper...

❖

So wrote Samuel Pepys in his diary more than three hundred years ago. In his day simply making the journey to Bath presented difficulties, as another diarist, Celia Fiennes, explained.

THENCE you pass a good way between 2 stone walls to the Bath 5 mile, down a very steep hill and stony a mile from the town scarce any passing and there descends a little current of water continually from the rocks; the wayes to the Bath are all difficult, the town lyes low in a bottom and its steep ascents all ways out of the town; the houses are indifferent, the streetes of a good size well pitched; there are severall good houses built for Lodgings that are new and adorned and good furniture, the baths in my opinion makes the town unpleasant, the aire thicke and hot by their steem, and by its own situation so low, encompassed with high hills and woods...

Not everyone was so disparaging about the setting of Bath. William Stukeley, the antiquary, was much more complimentary.

It is indeed a spot of ground which we Britons may esteem as a particular boon of Nature: it lies in a great valley surrounded with an amphitheatrical view of hills; and its situation on the west side of the island does not a little contribute to its pleasures; for such is ever less subject to violent and enormous alterations of the air by winds and tempest, heat and cold.

Pump Room and Abbey

For those who came frequently to Bath, and saw it in all its seasons, the variations of light and colour against its backcloth of hills was a source of recurring delight. The Victorian curate, Francis Kilvert, who lived nearby, recorded his impressions, in May, September, and November.

I THINK I never saw the beautiful city look lovelier than this morning in its early summer morning's dress, with the blue encircling hills climbed by crescents and terraces and the great Abbey towering above the river and looming across the river meads (6th May, 1871).

IT WAS A LOVELY MORNING, the clear shining after rain, and in the strange gauzy sunlit mist of the morning Bath looked like a beautiful mirage with a weird strange unearthly beauty, like an enchanted city (8th September, 1873).

THE MORNING was dull, thick and gloomy, threatening rain, but just before we got into Bath a sunbeam stole across the world and lighted the Queen of the West with the ethereal beauty of a fairy city, while all the land blazed gorgeous with the brilliant and many coloured trees. Almost in a moment the dull dark leaden sky was replaced by a sheet of brilliant blue and the lovely city shone dazzling and lustrous upon the hill sides, her palaces veiled with a tender mist and softened by delicate gleams of pearl and blue (2nd November, 1874).

The naturalist W.H. Hudson had a similar experience, which coloured his memories of Bath.

IT IS A TOWN built of white stone in the hollow of an oblong basin, with the River Avon flowing through it; and though perhaps too large for perfect beauty, it is exceedingly pleasant. Its 'stone walls do not a prison make', since they do not shut you out from rural sights and sounds: walking in almost any street, even in the lowest part, in the busiest, noisiest centre of the town, you have but to lift your eyes to see a green hill not far away; and viewed from the top of one of these hills that encircle it, Bath, in certain favourable states of the atmosphere, wears a beautiful look. One afternoon, a couple of miles out, I was on the top of Barrow Hill in a sudden, violent storm of rain and wind; when the rain ceased, the sun burst out behind me, and the town, rain-wet and sun-flushed, shone white as a city built of whitest marble against the green hills and black cloud on the farther side. Then on the slaty blackness appeared a complete and most brilliant rainbow, on one side streaming athwart the green hill and resting on the centre of the town, so that the high, old, richly-decorated Abbey Church was seen through a band of green and violet mist. That storm and that rainbow, seen by chance, gave a peculiar grace and glory to Bath, and the bright, unfading picture it left in memory has perhaps become too much associated in my mind with the thoughts of Bath, and has given me an exaggerated idea of its charm.

A Sense Of Harmony And Repose

Hudson, unlike Kilvert, was not a man who came regularly to Bath. But when he did, he found it a rejuvenating experience.

'TIS SO EASY to get from London to Bath, by merely stepping into a railway carriage which takes you smoothly without a stop in two short hours from Paddington, that I was amazed at myself in having allowed five full years to pass since my previous visit. The question was much in my mind as I strolled about noting the old-remembered names of streets and squares and crescents. Quiet Street was the name inscribed on one; it was, to me, the secret name of all. The old impressions were renewed, an old feeling partially recovered. The wide, clean ways; the solid, stone-built houses with their dignified aspect; the large distances, terrace beyond terrace; mansions and vast green lawns and parks and gardens; avenues and groups of stately trees, especially the unmatched clump of old planes in the Circus; the whole town, the design in the classic style of one master mind, set by the Avon, amid green hills, produced a sense of harmony and repose which cannot be equalled by any other town in the kingdom.

This idle time was delightful so long as I gave my attention exclusively to houses from the outside, and to hills, rocks, trees, waters, and all visible nature, which here harmonizes with man's works. To sit on some high hill and look down on Bath, sun-flushed or half veiled in mist; to lounge on Camden Crescent, or climb Sion Hill, or take my ease with the water-drinkers in the spacious, comfortable Pump Room; or, better still, to rest at noon in the ancient abbey - all this was pleasure pure and simple, a quiet drifting back until I found myself younger by five years than I had taken myself to be.

◆

J.B. Priestley, travelling through England in a motor-coach during the depressed 1930s, had a similar experience, which he expressed succinctly.

THEN Bath spread herself before us, like a beautiful dowager giving a reception. Bath, like Edinburgh, has the rare trick of surprising you all over again. You know very well it is like that, yet somehow your memory must have diminished the wonder of it, for there it is, taking your breath away again.

◆

But not everyone has felt that way about Bath. It rathers depends on the emotional luggage that you are carrying with you.

EVERYBODY has their taste in noises as well as in other matters; and sounds are quite innoxious, or most distressing, by their sort rather than their quantity. When Lady Russell, not long afterwards, was entering Bath on a wet afternoon, and driving through the long course of streets from the Old Bridge to Camden Place, amidst the dash of other carriages, the heavy rumble of carts and drays, the bawling of newsmen, muffinmen, and milkmen, and the ceaseless clink of pattens, she made no complaint. No, these were noises which belonged to the winter pleasures; her spirits rose under their influence; and, like Mrs Musgrove, she was feeling, though not saying, that, after being long in the country, nothing could be so good for her as a little quiet cheerfulness.

Anne did not share these feelings. She persisted in a very determined, though very silent, disinclination for Bath; caught the first dim view of the extensive buildings, smoking in rain, without any wish of seeing them better; felt their progress through the streets to be, however disagreeable, yet too rapid; for who would be glad to see her when she arrived?

❖

Jane Austen's penetrating eye saw the bittersweetness of Bath society. Horace Walpole, scribbling off unhappy letters from his lodgings, just felt bitter.

YES, THANK YOU, I am quite well again; and if I had not a mind to continue so, I would not remain here a day longer, for I am tired to death of the place... The elements certainly agree with me, but I shun the gnomes and salamanders, and have not once been at the rooms. Mr Chute stays with me till Tuesday. When he is gone, I do not know what I shall do, for I cannot play at cribbage by myself; and the alternative is to see my Lady Vane open the ball, and glimmer at fifty-four. All my comfort is, that I lodge close to the Cross Bath, by which means I avoid the Pump Room and all its works...

YOUR LADYSHIP ordered me to give you an account of myself, and I can give you a very good one. The waters agree with me as well as possible and do not heat me: all I have to complain of, is, that they have bestowed such an appetite on me, that I expect to return as fat as a hog, that is, something bigger than a lark. I hope this state of my health will content your Ladyship, and that you are not equally anxious about my pleasure, which does not go on quite so rapidly. I am tired to death of the place, and long to be at home, and grieve to lose such a delightful October. The waters agree so well with the trees in this country, that they have not a wrinkle or a yellow leaf, and the sun shines as brightly as it can possibly through such mists. I regret its beams being thrown away on such a dirty ditch as their river...

Lord Chatham has still a little gout in his arm, but takes the air. My Lord President goes to the balls, but I believe had rather go to the alehouse. Lady Vane, I hear, opens the balls, since it is too late for her now to go anywhere else. This is all I know of people I have not seen. As I shall not stay above a fortnight longer, I do not propose to learn the language... The Bath is sure of doing me some good, for I shall take great care of myself, for fear of being sent hither again.

It seems a very English trait, to persist in something disagreeable because it must be doing you good. Spectators, such as Samuel Richardson, found it fascinating.

IN THE BATH people stand up to the chin, men and women, and stew, mostly in the way of gallantry.

❖

That of course was not the Roman way. They were enthusiasts, and Bath was singled out in the third century for special mention by Solinus, a guidebook writer, in his 'Compendium of remarkable things'.

THE PERIMETER of Britain is forty-eight times seventy-five miles. Within this distance are rivers many and great, and hot springs equipped with sumptuous furnishings for the use of mankind. The presiding goddess of these springs is Minerva, and in her shrine the constant flames never whiten to ash, but as the fire subsides it turns to globules of stone.

In the medieval imagination it was not the Romans who first discovered the healing power of the Bath waters. The founder of Bath was Bladud, an ancient British king supposed to have been a contemporary of the Old Testament prophet Elijah. In this Elizabethan poem Bladud describes his discovery.

BY ARTS I made the holesome Baths at Bathe,
And made therefore two Tunnes of burning brasse:
And other twaine seven kinds of salts that have
In them inclosde, but these be made of glasse,
With sulphur fil'd, wilde fire emixt there was,
    And in foure welles these Tunnes I did assay,
    To place by arte that they might last of aye.

Which waters heate and clensing perfect powre,
With vapours of the sulphur, salts, and fire,
Hath vertue great, to heale, and wash, and scowre
The bathed sores therein that health desire.
If of the vertues, moe thou dost require,
    I will recite what old experience telles,
    In causes cold the vertues of these welles.

The bathes to soften sinewes vertue have,
And also for to clense and scowre the skin
From Morphewes white and blacke, to heale and save
The bodies freckled, faint, are bath'd therein:
Scabs, lepry, sores both old and festered in,

The scurfe, botch, itch, gout, poxe, and humors fell,
    The milt and liver hard it healeth well.

I must confesse by learned skill I found
Those native welles whence ye have helpe for men.
But well thou know'st there runnes from under ground
Springs sweet, salt, cold, and hote even now as then,
From rocke, salt-petre, alume, gravell, fen,
    From sulphur, iron, lead, gold, brasse and tinne:
    Springs vertue take of vaines that they been in.

Then who so knowes by natures worke in these,
Of metals or of mines the force to heale,
May sooner give his iudgement in disease,
For curing by the bath, and surer deale
With sickly people of the publique weale,
    And also find of fountaines hot, and cold,
    To heale by them the sicke, both yong and old.

The Citie eke of Bathe, I founded there,
Renouned far by reason of the wels:
And many monuments that ancient were
I placed there, thou know'st the storie tels.
I sought renowne and fame and nothing els.
    But when our actes extols us to the skies,
    We look not downe from whence we first did rise.

◆

By the time those words were written scholars had begun to doubt the magic powers of Bladud. John Rastell, in 1529, expressed a deal of scepticism, but his more 'scientific' explanation does not come across as very convincing.

BLADUD son of Ludibras reynyd next he made the cyte of Bath & as the story seyth he was a grete nigromancyer and by the craft made there the hote bathys but other clerkis hold opynyon that they come naturally of the grounde be cause ther be manny sych in other placis as in darbyshyer at boxtone and many other in Italye and dyvers other landis some phylozophers holde that the cause thereof is thus that wha' there is a hote fume which perpetuall comyth and fumyth out of the yerth whereof ye may se manny of them by experyence in Italy which be ever perpetually hote and fumyng and smokyng out of the yerth lyke wyse as wel spryngis come out of the yerth perpetually. & when anny welspryng brekyth out at any place of the yerth where sych a hote fume is nygh Joyni'g tha' if th't hote fume be bygger of power the' it will naturally make the water hote and because th't hote fume and welspryng be both of theyr naturis perpetuall that hote bath of water must be perpetually hote but whether man will beleve the history or the phylozophers every man is at his lyberte. This Bladud reynyd xxi yere.

◆

The scientists of the seventeenth century had begun to analyse the waters, and to experiment with drinking it. But still they were not sure why it was hot.

OUR BATH WATERS consist of: 1. Bitumen, which hath the predominancy; sovereign to discuss, glutinate, dissolve, open obstructions, &c. 2. Nitre, which dilateth the bitumen, making the solution the better, the water the clearer. It cleanseth and purgeth both by stool and urine, cutteth and disolveth gross humours. 3. Sulphur, in regard whereof they dry, resolve, mollify, attract, and are good for uterine effects, proceeding from cold and windy humours.

But how these waters came by their great heat is rather controverted than concluded amongst the learned. Some impute it to wind, or airy exhalations, included in the bowels of the earth, which by their agitation and attrition (upon the rocks and narrow passages) gather heat, and impart it to the waters.

They are used also inwardly, in broths, beer, juleps, &c., with good effect. And although some mislike it, because they will not mix medicaments with aliments, yet such practice beginneth to prevail.

❖

Scientific and medical opinion about the origin and uses of the waters had developed in various picturesque ways by the time of Samuel Richardson's exposition in 1742.

THE BATH WATERS certainly owe their heat to a mixture and fermentation of two different sources, distilling from the tops of two different mountains (Clarton and Landsdown) meeting in the valley where the town stands; for all hills are nests of metals or minerals, and their bellies are cavernous and hollow. It is not therefore improbable, that on Clarton Down there should lie the sulphurous matter which must rise by impregnation from that excellent stone quarry, which hardens in the air, and grows cased with a nitrous coat by time, and cold weather, and is so readily cut out and carved into any the most exquisite shapes. This the discovery and property of the worthy, charitable, and pious Ralph Allen, Esq. For all mineral waters owe their virtue to an impregnation of rain water, generated from the clouds, which are compressed in their course by mountains or eminences, and fall on the respective included mineral. And every one knows, that a due mixture of sulphur, and filings of iron, moistened with water, will produce any degree of heat. This quarry therefore must have a large quantity of sulphurous or bituminous matter in its composition, as will be evident to a natural philosopher, from these mentioned qualities of the stone. Neither is it improbable, that the ferruginous or iron-tinctured water takes its rise from Lansdown Quarry, the stone on it being hard, and on the top flinty, black, and acrimonious, as iron ore is known to be. These two mountains, thus tinged by rain water falling from the proper heights, meet in some caverns in the valley; and, there fermenting produce that hot, milky, soft, salutiferous beverage, called Bath water, far beyond any hot mineral waters for its delicacy, and supportable, tho' comfortable heat, to any other such water hitherto discovered on the habitable globe, as it possesses that milkiness, detergency, and middling heat so friendly adapted to weaken'd animal constitutions, which all other hot waters want in the due degree; either being too hot, or too cold, to do any great good in cases where they are proper. These waters are beneficial in almost all chronical distempers, and can hurt in none, except in hemorrhages, inflammations, or bad lungs, unless they be over-dosed in quantity, or too high and too hot a regimen be joined with them; for they always procure a great appetite, and good spirits, if cautiously managed; but if high meats, and strong liquors, be indulged, they will create inflammatory disorders. However, in weak stomachs, decayed appetites, colicks, low spirits, in the intervals of the fits of the gout and stone; in rheumatisms, palsies, nervous disorders; and, in a word, all those called the cold diseases; but most eminently, in all the disorders of the chyliferous tube, or the stomach and belly not inflamed, they are more kindly and beneficial than any medicine known in nature; and introduce a natural warmth, and a new internal heat, into decayed, worn-out, superannuated constitutions; and if a light regimen, due exercise, and good hours, be joined with them, they would truly work wonders.

Indeed, the traveller and antiquary William Stukeley had tried it for himself.

THE CORPORATION has lately erected a pretty handsome building before it, called the Drinking-room, for the company to meet in that drink the waters drawn hither by a marble pump from the bottom of the springs, where it is near boiling hot. This water is admirably grateful to the stomach, striking the roof of the mouth with a fine sulphureous and steely gas, like that of the German Spa or Pyrmont: though you drink off a large pint glass, yet it is so far from creating a heaviness, or nausea, that you find yourself brisker immediately, by its agreeable sensation on the membranes of the stomach: at first it operates by stool, and especially urine: it is of most sovereign virtue to strengthen the bowels, to restore their lost tone through intemperance or inactivity, and renews the vital fire by its adventitious heat and congenial principles. Hither let the hypochondriac student repair, and drink at the Muses' spring: no doubt the advantages obtained here in abdominal obstructions must be very great.

◆

It was a taste which lingered in the memory, and not everyone was impressed by it.

'HAVE you drank the waters, Mr Weller?' inquired his companion, as they walked towards High Street.

'Once,' replied Sam.

'What did you think of 'em, sir?'

'I thought they wos particklery unpleasant,' replied Sam.

'Ah,' said Mr John Smauker, 'you dislike the killibeate taste, perhaps?'

'I don't know much about that 'ere,' said Sam. 'I thought they's a wery strong flavour o' warm flat irons.'

'That *is* the killibeate, Mr Weller,' observed Mr John Smauker, comtemptuously.

'Well, if it is, it's a wery inexpressive word, that's all,' said Sam. 'It may be, but I ain't much in the chimical line myself, so I can't say.' And here, to the great horror of Mr John Smauker, Sam Weller began to whistle.

Dickens was not the only novelist to criticize the water. Tobias Smollett had practised as a physician in Bath during the 1750s, and knew at first hand that the treatment might kill rather than cure.

DISEASED persons of all ages, sexes, and conditions, are promiscuously admitted into an open Bath, which affords little or no shelter from the inclemencies of the weather, such as wind, rain, hail, and snow: for, by the peculiar sagacity of the learned in that place, the bathing time is limited to the most severe season of the year. This being the case, it may be reasonably supposed, that many of the fair sex are withheld by modesty from going into the Bath, where they must not only mingle with male patients, to whose persons and complaints they are utter strangers; but, likewise, be exposed in a very mortifying point of view, to the eyes of all the company, in the Pump-room, as well as to those of the footmen and common people, whose curiosity leads them to look over the walls of the Bath: some may be apprehensive of being tainted with infectious distempers; or disgusted with the nauseating appearances of the filth, which, being washed from the bodies of the patients, is left sticking to the sides of the place.

Although the king's and queen's Baths have been known to contain five-and-forty patients at one time, the number of guides does not exceed half a dozen of each sex; so that if any of those Bathers who are unattended should be seized with a sudden Vertigo, fit, or other accident, they might lose their lives for want of proper assistance. But, granting no such accident should happen, some of them, on retiring from the Bath, must, from this defect in point of attendance, remain in the wet bathing dress, until their constitutions are greatly endangered. This inconvenience is rendered more grievous by the nature of that dress, which, being made of canvas, grows cold and clammy in a moment, and clings to the surface of the body with a most hazardous adhesion. If they should escape the consequences of both these risques, they may still be subject to another, in being obliged to wait in a cold slip for their respective chairs, which cannot always be brought to them in proper time, because the passage is freqently blocked up. After all, they are carried to their lodgings, while their pores are open from the effects of the Bath, in paultry chairs made of slight cross bars of wood, fastened together with girth web, covered with bays, and, for the most part, destitute of lining; these machines, by standing in the street till called for, are often rendered so damp by the weather, that the Bathers cannot use them without imminent hazard of their lives.

Lansdown Road

Smollett's criticisms did not endear him to his fellow-physicians in Bath, and he soon left to pursue his literary career. At the end of his life his vendetta against the Bath waters (as expressed by one of his characters) took a savage — and nauseating — turn.

BUT I AM NOW as much afraid of drinking, as of bathing; for, after a long conversation with the Doctor, about the construction of the pump and the cistern, it is very far from being clear with me, that the patients in the Pump-room don't swallow the scourings of the bathers. I can't help suspecting, that there is, or may be, some regurgitation from the bath into the cistern of the pump. In that case, what a delicate beveridge is every day quaffed by the drinkers; medicated with the sweat and dirt, and dandriff; and the abominable discharges of various kinds, from twenty different diseased bodies, parboiling in the kettle below. In order to avoid this filthy composition, I had recourse to the spring that supplies the private baths on the Abbey-green; but I at once perceived something extraordinary, in the taste and smell; and, upon inquiry, I find that the Roman baths in this quarter, were found covered by an old burying ground, belonging to the Abbey; through which, in all probability, the water drains in its passage, so that as we drink the decoction of living bodies at the Pump-room, we swallow the strainings of rotten bones and carcasses at the private bath - I vow to God, the very idea turns my stomach! - Determined as I am, against any farther use of the Bath waters, this consideration would give me little disturbance, if I could find any thing more pure, or less pernicious, to quench my thirst; but, although the natural springs of excellent water are seen gushing spontaneous on every side, from the hills that surround us, the inhabitants, in general, make use of well-water, so impregnated with nitre, or alum, or some other villainous mineral, that it is equally ungrateful to the taste, and mischievous to the constitution. It must be owned, indeed, that here, in Milsham-street, we have a precarious and scanty supply from the hill; which is collected in an open bason in the Circus, liable to be defiled with dead dogs, cats, rats, and every species of nastiness, which the rascally populace may throw into it, from mere wantonness and brutality.

◆

Ugghh! But Smollett was not the only one to express scepticism about the curative properties of the Bath waters. Here is Cam Hobhouse taking a swipe at the doctors, the cures, and the patients altogether.

IT SOUNDS rather strange, but I tell you no lie,
There's many good people that come here to die;
For the London practitioners wisely declare,
When their patients can't breathe, they must try change
                                           of air.
Says Sir Walter – "Dear Lady, I thought all the while,
"That dropsy of yours must proceed from the bile;
"The waters of Bath have made wonderful cures

"Of many I know, in such cases as yours,
"You'll go down directly to Bath, if you're wise."
So down goes my Lady directly – and dies.
"To tell her the truth of the case would have shock'd her,
"But, thank heav'n, she's off of my hands," says the doctor...
Such cases are frequent, and yet not a few
Come here to be ill, just for something to do.
Then, too, we've the nervous, as David observes,
What would come of the doctors, except for the nerves?
These delicate creatures, they feel no aversion
To join with the rest in the gen'ral diversion.
Each morning the medical gentleman calls,
Each evening my Lady stands up at the balls:
What with parties and routs, ere the season is ended,
At last she becomes what at first she pretended.

❖

Despite all this, some of the patients made prodigious recoveries.

MATTHEW BENNET, of Clifton in the County of Warwick, Shoemaker, in an Hemiplegia, or Half-Palsey, of the Right Side, with many Cramps, and frequent Convulsive Motions of the Muscles of the Mouth, Arms, and other Parts, especially of the Fingers of the left Hand, after 12 Days Bathing, at one Season in the Hot (or Long) Bath, and 3

Weeks at another, received Cure, 23 May, 1677.

Note, That these Convulsions were from Emptiness, by Reason of Weakness and Defect of the Animal Spirits, and those we call Symptomatic, which, on the Cure of the Palsey, vanished; whereas the convulsive Motions called Essential, or depending on no other Diseases, by the Use of the Hotter Waters, and the Hot-Bath particularly, are usually provoked.

MR THOMAS BROOKES, Minister of the Word of God in London, 60 Years of Age, having his Head and Original of the Nerves ill affected, and 16 Years a gravative Pain in the Back and Kidneys, came to Bath 1679, where, Preparatories premised, he drank the Waters from the Dry-Pump at the King's Bath, in a due Method and Order directed by me, and voided a great Quantity of a very fine Powder, which subsided in the Bottom of the Urinal, which the Urine evaporated *ad siccitatem*, made Eight Pills as big as Pistol Bullets, of the Colour and Consistence of Stone, and at his return home, evacuated as much more of that fine Powder resembling Flower, as would make 44 Pills more, without Mixture of any thing to make 'em up. All the Matter together, voided in no long Time, was enough to make a Ball of Stone of Six Ounces Weight; which coming away, the heavy Pain in the Kidneys and Back afterwards ceased; but the Patient having many Diseases besides, after a Year's Time, or thereabouts, departed this Life.

'Tis here to be noted, That the small Stones were of equal Hardness with Marble, and being dapped on the Ground would rebound into the Hand, like those the Boys use to play with, and call Marbles... I saw these stone Pills or globular Concretions not at all relented, as hard as ever, seven Years after they had been voided in Powder.

MR JAMES HOW, of London, about 40 Years of Age, troubled with the Spleen, and consequently an ill Disposition of the Stomach, and Guts, occasioning a bad Retention of Food, and faulty Chyle, whence a Want of Appetite, an Atrophy, and thin Habit of Body, with great Impair of Strength did proceed. There was also an undue Fermentation of the Juices issuing from the Sweetbread and Bladder of Gall, and sometimes so great a Working of contrary Matter, that sharp and flatulent Humours, making their Way upwards and downwards, gave Torments to the Bowels, and created in the Stomach a Nauseousness, Vomiting, and great Distension from Wind.

After many Remedies from divers Physicians, in the Month of June 1681 he came to Bath, where the Bath not so well agreeing with him, I advised him to drink the Water, upon which at first, by reason of the stubborn rebellious Nature of the Humours, he grew much worse: But in some time after, taking the Water in lesser Quantities, longer Distances, and fasting thereupon, the Vomiting and Reaching went off, the Bowels became strong, and a good Habit of Body appeared, so that now enjoying a very good Appetite he can eat two or three times in a Day, digest well, distribute good Chyle, and perform all the Functions and Offices of Nature to best Advantage.

So beneficial had Bath water become that it could cure even the well.

... IN THREE DAYS' TIME they were all located in their new abode, when Mr Pickwick began to drink the waters with the utmost assiduity. Mr Pickwick took them systematically. He drank a quarter of a pint before breakfast, and then walked up a hill; and another quarter of a pint after breakfast, and then walked down a hill; and after every fresh quarter of a pint, Mr Pickwick declared, in the most solemn and emphatic terms, that he felt a great deal better: whereat his friends were very much delighted, though they had not been previously aware that there was anything the matter with him.

❖

Mr Pickwick, in the 1830s, was following a long-established tradition. Daniel Defoe had observed its beginnings, more than a century earlier.

BUT NOW we may say it is the resort of the sound, rather than the sick; the bathing is made more a sport and a diversion, than a physical prescription for health; and the town is taken up in raffling, gameing, visiting, and in a word, all sorts of gallantry and levity.

A Bath Assortment

But if the physical ills were set discreetly to one side, others -— social ills — arrived to take their place. First there was the problem of servants.

O MOLLY! the sarvants at Bath are devils in garnet - They lite the candle at both ends - Here's nothing but ginketting, and wasting, and thieving and tricking, and trigging; and then they are never content - They won't suffer the squire and mistress to stay any longer; because they have been already above three weeks in the house; and they look for a couple of ginneys a-piece at our going away; and this is a parquisite they expect every month in the season; being as how no family has a right to stay longer than four weeks in the same lodgings; and so the cuck swears she will pin the dish-clout to mistress's tail, and the house-maid vows, she'll put cowitch in master's bed, if so be he don't discamp without furder ado - I don't blame them for making the most of their market, in the way of vails and parquisites; and I defy the devil to say I am a tail-carrier, or ever brought a poor sarvant into trouble - But then they oft to have some conscience, in vronging those that be sarvants like themselves - For you must no, Molly, I missed three-quarters of blond lace, and a remnant of muslin, and my silver thimble; which was the gift of true love; they were all in my work-basket, that I left upon the table in the sarvants-hall, when mistresses bell rung; but if they had been under lock and kay, 'twould have been all the same, for there are double keys to all the locks in Bath; and they say as how the very teeth an't safe in your head, if you sleep with your mouth open.

Actually, rampant dishonesty in Bath was nothing new. The Roman curses scratched on lead tablets and thrown into the sacred spring by vengeful victims are eloquent witness of that.

SOLINUS to the goddess Sulis Minerva. I give to your divinity and majesty my bathing tunic and cloak. Do not allow sleep or health to him who has done me wrong, whether man or woman, whether slave or free, unless he reveals himself and brings those goods to your temple...

THE PERSON who has lifted my bronze vessel is utterly accursed. I give him to the temple of Sulis, whether woman or man, whether slave or free, whether boy or girl, and let him who has done this spill his own blood into the vessel himself...

BASILIA gives in to the temple of Mars her silver ring, that so long as someone, whether slave or free, has been privy or knows anything about it, he may be accursed in his blood and eyes and every limb, or even have all his intestines quite eaten away, if he has stolen the ring or been privy to the theft.

❖

Light-fingered slaves and grasping servants were not the only problems which a genteel visitor to Bath might try to avoid.

'THIS is a ball-night,' said the M.C., again taking Mr Pickwick's hand, as he rose to go. 'The ball-nights in Ba-ath are moments snatched from Paradise; rendered bewitching by music, beauty, elegance, fashion, etiquette, and – and – above all, by the absence of tradespeople, who are quite inconsistent with Paradise; and who have an amalgamation of themselves at the Guildhall every fortnight, which is, to say the least, remarkable. Good bye, good bye!' and protesting all the way downstairs that he was most satisfied, and most delighted, and most overpowered, and most flattered, Angelo Cyrus Bantam, Esquire, M.C., stepped into a very elegant chariot that waited at the door, and rattled off.

◆

Which was the more objectionable, one wonders — the remarkable tradesmen, or that obsequious villain, the Master of Ceremonies? But for some Bath visitors, such as Smollett's Jery Melford, it was the confusion of classes which provided the entertainment.

HERE, for example, a man has daily opportunities of seeing the most remarkable characters of the community. He sees them in their natural attitudes and true colours;

descended from their pedestals, and divested of their formal draperies, undisguised by art and affectation - Here we have ministers of state, judges, generals, bishops, projectors, philosophers, wits, poets, players, chemists, fiddlers, and buffoons. If he makes any considerable stay in the place, he is sure of meeting with some particular friend, whom he did not expect to see; and to me there is nothing more agreeable than such casual rencounters - Another entertainment, peculiar to Bath, arises from the general mixture of all degrees assembled in our public rooms, without distinction of rank or fortune. This is what my uncle reprobates, as a monstrous jumble of heterogeneous principles; a vile mob of noise and impertinence, without decency or subordination. But this chaos is to me a source of infinite amusement.

It amused Jane Austen, too. And she could portray snobbery with savage precision.

'HOW is Mary?' said Elizabeth; and without waiting for an answer, 'And, pray, what brings the Crofts to Bath?'
'They come on the admiral's account. He is thought to be gouty.'

'Gout and decrepitude!' said Sir Walter. 'Poor old gentleman!'

'Have they any acquaintance here?' asked Elizabeth.

'I do not know; but I can hardly suppose that, at Admiral Croft's time of life, and in his profession, he should not have many acquaintance in such a place as this.'

'I suspect,' said Sir Walter coolly, 'that Admiral Croft will be best known in Bath as the renter of Kellynch Hall. — Elizabeth, may we venture to present him and his wife in Laura Place?'

'Oh no, I think not. Situated as we are with Lady Dalrymple, cousins, we ought to be very careful not to embarrass her with acquaintance she might not approve. If we were not related, it would not signify; but as cousins she would feel scrupulous as to any proposal of ours. We had better leave the Crofts to find their own level. There are several odd-looking men walking about here who, I am told, are sailors. The Crofts will associate with them.'

◆

At first, when Bath's popularity began to grow, the niceties of social behaviour were lost on the visitors. And the accommodation was equally lacking in sophistication.

STILL however, the amusements of this place were neither elegant, nor conducted with delicacy. General society among people of rank or fortune was by no means established. The nobility still preserved a tincture of Gothic haughtiness, and refused to keep company with the gentry at any of the public entertainments of the place. Smoking in the rooms was permitted; gentlemen and ladies appeared in a disrespectful manner at public entertainments in aprons and boots. With an eagerness common to those, whose pleasures come but seldom, they generally continued them too long, and thus they were rendered disgusting by too free an enjoyment. If the company liked each other they danced till morning, if any person lost at cards, he insisted on continuing the game till luck should turn. The lodgings for visitants were paltry, though expensive, the dining rooms and other chambers were floored with boards coloured brown with soot and small beer, to hide the dirt; the walls were covered with unpainted wainscot, the furniture corresponded with the meanness of the architecture; a few oak chairs, a small looking glass, with a fender and tongs, composed the magnificence of these temporary habitations. The city was in itself mean and contemptible, no elegant buildings, no open streets, nor uniform squares.

◆

That was the sophisticated Oliver Goldsmith, looking back on the benighted city before Beau Nash civilized it. But at the time it did not seem so bad. Celia Fiennes, the indomitable horsewoman, paid her visit some twenty years before the Beau arrived, and she rather enjoyed her Bath.

THE PLACES for divertion about the Bath is either the walkes in that they call the Kings Mead, which is a pleasant green meaddow, where are walkes round and cross it, no place for coaches, and indeed there is little use of a coach only to bring and carry the Company from the Bath for the wayes are not proper for coaches, the town and all its accomodations is adapted to the batheing and drinking of the waters, and to nothing else, the streetes are well pitched and cleane kept and there are Chaires as in London to carry the better sort of people in visits, or if sick or infirme, and is only in the town, for its so encompassed with high hills few care to take the aire on them; there is also pleasant walkes in the Cathedrall in the Cloysters...

There are green walkes very pleasant and in many places, and out of the Cathedrall you walk in to the Priory which has good walkes of rows of trees which is plesant; there are the deans, prebends and doctors houses which stand in that green, which is pleasant, by the Church called the Abby which is lofty and spacious, and much Company walke there especially in wet weather; the Quire is neat but nothing extraordinary; in that Kings Mead there are severall little Cake-houses where you have fruit Sulibubs and sum'er liquours to entertaine the Company that walke there.

The markets are very good here of all sorts of provision flesh and fish, especially when the season for the Company batheing and drinking lasts, great plenty and pretty reasonable; the chargeableness of the Bath is the lodgings and firing, the faggotts being very small but they give you very good attendance there.

As more and more people resorted to Bath it became a bit of a squash to fit them all in. And there was a litter problem.

THE WALLS are almost intire, and perhaps the work of the Romans, except the upper part, which seems repaired with the ruins of Roman buildings; for the lewis-holes are still left in many of the stones, and, to the shame of the repairers, many Roman inscriptions, some sawn across, to fit the size of the place. The level of the city is risen to the top of the first walls, thro' the negligence of the magistracy, who, in this, and all other great towns, connive at the servants throwing dirt and ashes into the streets. These walls inclose but a small compass, of a pentagonal form. There are four gates on four sides, and a postern on the other.. The small compass of the city has made the inhabitants croud up the streets to an unseemly and inconvenient narrowness. It is, however, handsomely built, mostly of new stone, which is very white and good.

Pulteney Bridge

After the waters, its stone was Bath's greatest asset. Ralph Allen, the city's postmaster and a great entrepreneur, purchased the quarry from which much of the stone came, and so made his fortune. Not only in Bath, but all over England, the remarkable freestone embellished streets and buildings. The business became a tourist attraction in its own right.

THE RIVER AVON runs by the back of the town; and on the banks of it, Mr Allen, who is the genius of the place, and whose works and inventions there, next to the waters, are better worth the attention of the curious, than any thing in Bath, has a fine wharf, and other convenient places, to shape, to work, to imbark the stones of many tons weight, which he digs from the quarry, on the adjacent hill. This he does by an admirable machine, which runs down the hill by grooves placed in the ground, without horses or any other help, than one man to guide it, who also by a particular spring can stop it in the steepest part of the hill, and in the swiftest part of its motion. These stones he can carry by the Avon to Bristol, whence they may be transported to any other part of England.

So spectacular was the stones' descent that Mr Allen and his contraption even made a guest appearance in one of those characteristically florid and Muse-infested poems of the period.

NOW leave the Terrace, and th' extended Scene
Of Hills inclos'd, and Meadows ever-green.
Descend to Walks, 'twixt Limes in adverse Rows,
And view the gay Parterre, that ever blows.
This fair Pavilion view; around its Base
Observe the sporting of the scaly Race.
A cool Recess, the Muses chosen Seat,
From Crouds, and empty Noise, a blest Retreat!
The lovely Landscape, and the silent Stream,
Inspire the Poet, and present the Theme.
Round the green Walk the River glides away,
Where 'midst Espaliers balmy Zephyrs play,
And fan the Leaves, and cool the scorching Ray;
View the brown Shadows of yon pathless Wood,
And craggy Hills, irregular and rude!
Where Nature sports romantic: Hence is seen
The new-made Road, and wonderful Machine,
Self-moving downward from the Mountain's Height,
A Rock its Burden, of a Mountain's Weight.
Hail mighty Genius! born for great Designs,
T'adorn your Country, and to mend the Times;
Virtue's Exemplar in degen'rate Days,
All who love Virtue, love to speak your Praise.
You chide the Muse that dares your Virtues own,

And, veil'd with Modesty, would live unknown;
An honest Muse, no Prostitute for Gain,
Int'rest may court her, but shall court in vain:
But ever pleas'd to set true Worth in View,
Yours shall be seen, and will, by All but You.

◆

Mary Chandler, the deservedly obscure poetess, was quite right to point out that Ralph Allen's stone was everywhere to be seen. By the 1730s the pace of new building in Bath seems to have been frenetic, as Samuel Richardson pointed out.

THE BATH-STONE, which I have mention'd before, affords a fine opportunity to imbellish and give a noble look to the buildings here, and at a very cheap rate; for the front of the houses on the north side of the square cost no more than £500 tho' it is above 200 feet in extent, and inriched with columns and pilasters in the Corinthian Order. All the danger is, that they will over-build themselves now they are got into the humour, and make it less worth while to those who let lodgings, the principal business of the place; but then people of fortune, settling there, will make amends for it; since no less than 70 or 80 families are already become constant inhabitants, and others are daily taking houses.

◆

The city continued, sporadically at least, throughout the eighteenth century to resemble a vast building site. And while it was going on, the ordered terraces and crescents which we so much enjoy seemed to an onlooker to be a hopeless jumble. Here is part of a letter from Bath, written by Fanny Burney in 1791.

THIS CITY is so filled with Workmen, dust and lime, that you really want two pair of Eyes to walk about in it, — one for being put out, and the other to see with afterwards. But as I, however, have only one pair, which are pretty much dedicated to the first purpose, you cannot, in reason, expect from me a very distinct description of it. Bath seems now, rather a collection of small Towns, or of magnificent Villas, than one City. They are now building as if the World was but just beginning, and this was the only spot on which its Inhabitants could endure to reside. Nothing is secure from their architectural rage. They build upon the pinnacle of Hills that only to look up to breaks ones neck, - and they build in the deepest depths below, which only to look down upon makes one giddy. Even the streets round the Pump room are pulling down for new Edifices, and you can only drink from their choice stream, by wading through their chosen mud. Their plans seem all to be formed without the least reference to what adjoins or surrounds them, they are therefore high, low, broad, narrow, long, short, in manners the most unexpected, and by interruptions the most abrupt; - and some of their Houses are placed so zig-zag, in and out, you would suppose them built first, and then dropt, to find their own foundation. They seem seldom to attempt levelling the Ground for the sake of uniformity, but, very contentedly, when they have raised one House on the spot where it could stand most conveniently, they raise the next upon its nearest and steepest aclivity, so precisely above it, that from the Garret of one, you Mount into the Kitchen of the other. One street, leading out of Laura Place, of a noble width, and with a broad handsome Pavement, pompously labelled at the corner Johnson Street, has in it - only one House: - nor can another be added, for it opens to Spring Gardens, and even its *vis a vis* is occupied by the dead wall belonging to a house in Laura Place. Nor can you make a visit from one street to another, without such an ascent, or such a declivity, that you must have the wheel of a carriage locked to go from neighbour to neighbour.- You will ask me if I mean to set you up with materials for making a model of Bath? but I am perfectly content with having given you a Model of Confusion.

Certainly, unless you are advised to come hither for Health, I should advise you not to see the place these 2 years, at least, for pleasure; as the avenues to the Pump Rooms will not sooner be finished, and walking here in the winter must be next to impracticable. However, when all these works are compleated, and the Compleaters, with the usual gratitude of the world, are driven aloof, this City, already the most splendid of England, will be as noble as can well be conceived.

Bath Abbey

In truth, the ennobling of Bath, like the building of Bath, had been in progress for most of the eighteenth century. And while Ralph Allen and Bath's famous architects, John Wood senior and junior, were attending to the correct orders of the architecture, Richard ('Beau') Nash was working on the principles of correct behaviour.

RULES to be observ'd at BATH

1. That a visit of ceremony at first coming, and another at going away, are all that are expected or desired, by ladies of quality and fashion, - except impertinents.

2. That ladies coming to the ball appoint a time for their footmen coming to wait on them home, to prevent disturbance and inconveniencies to themselves and others.

3. That gentlemen of fashion never appearing in a morning before the ladies in gowns and caps, shew breeding and respect.

4. That no person take it ill that any one goes to another's play, or breakfast, and not theirs; - except captious by nature.

5. That no gentleman give his ticket for the balls,

to any but gentlewomen. - N.B. Unless he has none of his acquaintance.

6. That gentlemen crowding before the ladies at the ball, shew ill manners; and that none do so for the future, - except such as respect nobody but themselves.

7. That no gentleman or lady takes it ill that another dances before them; - except such as have no pretence to dance at all.

8. That the elder ladies and children be content with a second bench at the ball, as being past or not come to perfection.

9. That the younger ladies take notice how many eyes observe them. N.B. This does not extend to the Have-at-alls [female gamblers].

10. That all whisperers of lies and scandals, be taken for their authors.

11. That all repeaters of such lies, and scandal be shun'd by all company; - except such as have been guilty of the same crime. N.B. Several men of no character, old women and young ones, of question'd reputation, are great authors of lies in this place, being of the sect of levellers.

When everybody understood the rules, and behaved accordingly, then the proceedings, with Beau Nash in charge, would run like clockwork.

THE BALLS by his direction were to begin at six, and to end at eleven. Nor would he suffer them to continue a moment longer, lest invalids might commit irregularities, to counteract the benefit of the waters. Every thing was to be performed in proper order. Each ball was to open with a minuet, danced by two persons of the highest distinction present. When the minuet concluded, the lady was to return to her seat, and Mr Nash was to bring the gentleman a new partner. This ceremony was to be observed by every succeeding couple, every gentleman being obliged to dance with two ladies till the minuets were over, which generally continued two hours. At eight the country dances were to begin, ladies of quality, according to their rank, standing up first. About nine o' clock a short interval was allowed for rest, and for the gentlemen to help their partners to tea. That over, the company were to pursue their amusements till the clock struck eleven. Then the master of the ceremonies entering the ball-room, ordered the music to desist by lifting up his finger. The dances discontinued, and some time allowed for becoming cool, the ladies were handed to their chairs.

❖

Anyone who put a foot wrong was administered a swift reprimand.

'ANYBODY HERE?' inquired Dowler suspiciously.
'Anybody! The elite of Ba-ath. Mr Pickwick, do you see the lady in the gauze turban?'
'The fat old lady?' inquired Mr Pickwick, innocently.
'Hush, my dear sir - nobody's fat or old in Ba-ath. That's the Dowager Lady Snuphanuph.'
'Is it indeed?' said Mr Pickwick.

◆

And that is what the whole elaborate charade was directed towards — ladies and gentlemen, men and women, young and not-so-young, eyeing one another up and trying to impress. It was the game that everyone was there to play, and had been playing long before Beau Nash.

AND SO BIFEL that ones in a Lente-
So often tymes I to my gossyb wente,
For evere yet I loved to be gay,
And for to walke in March, Averill, and May,
Fro hous to hous, to heere sondry talys-
That Jankyn clerk and my gossyb dame Alys
And I myself into the feeldes wente.
Myn housbonde was at Londoun al the Lente;
I hadde the bettre leyser for to pleye,
And for to se, and eek for to be seye
Of lusty folk. What wiste I wher my grace

Was shapen for to be, or in what place?
Therfore I made my visitaciouns
To vigilies and to processiouns,
To prechyng eek, and to thise pilgrimages,
To pleye of myracles, and to mariages,
And wered upon my gaye scarlet gytes-
Thise wormes, ne thise motthes, ne thise mytes,
Upon my peril, frete hem never a deel;
And wostow why? For they were used weel.

    Now wol I tellen forth what happed me.
I seye that in the feeldes walked we,
Til trewely we hadde swich daliance,
This clerk and I, that of my purveiance
I spak to hym and seyde hym how that he,
If I were wydwe, sholde wedde me.
For certeinly, I sey for no bobance,
Yet was I nevere withouten purveiance
Of mariage, n'of othere thynges eek.
I holde a mouses herte nat worth a leek
That hath but oon hole for to sterte to,
And if that faille, thanne is al ydo.

    I bar hym on honde he hadde enchanted me-
My dame taughte me that soutiltee.
And eek I seyde I mette of hym al nyght;
He wolde han slayn me as I lay upright,
And al my bed was ful of verray blood,
But yet I hope that he shal do me good,
For blood bitokeneth gold, as me was taught-
And al was fals; I dremed of it right naught,

> But I folwed ay my dames loore,
> As wel of this as of othere thynges moore.

◆

Chaucer's Wife of Bath was an expert. So was Defoe's Moll Flanders, three centuries later.

THE LOOKING after my cargo of goods soon after obliged me to take a journey to Bristol, and during my attendance upon that affair I took the diversion of going to the Bath, for as I was still far from being old, so my humour, which was always gay, continued so to an extreme. and being now, as it were, a woman of fortune, though I was a woman without a fortune, I expected something or other might happen in my way that might mend my circumstances, as had been my case before.

The Bath is a place of gallantry enough; expensive, and full of snares. I went thither, indeed, in the view of taking anything that might offer, but I must do myself that justice, as to protest I knew nothing amiss; I meant nothing but in an honest way, nor had I any thoughts about me at first that looked the way which afterwards I suffered them to be guided.

Here I stayed the whole latter season, as it is called there, and contracted some unhappy acquaintance, which rather prompted the follies I fell afterwards into than fortified me against them. I lived pleasantly enough, kept good company, that is to say, gay, fine company; but had the discouragement to find this way of living sunk me exceedingly, and that as I had no settled income, so spending upon the main stock was but a certain kind of bleeding to death; and this gave me many sad reflections in the intervals of my other thoughts. However, I shook them off, and still flattered myself that something or other might offer for my advantage.

But I was in the wrong place for it. I was not now at Redriff, where, if I had set myself tolerably up, some honest sea captain or other might have talked with me upon the honourable terms of matrimony; but I was at the Bath, where men find a mistress sometimes, but very rarely look for a wife; and consequently all the particular acquaintances a woman can expect to make there must have some tendency that way.

◆

Moll, by the time she reached Bath, had learned to be sanguine about such matters. There were always plenty of men eyeing up the ladies, as Cam Hobhouse observed.

> SUPPOSING, dear dunce! that you've nothing to do,
> You'll get up at one, and you'll walk out at two.
> There's something quite pleasant in walking the streets,
> For the sights that one sees, and the friends that one meets:
> The ladies of Bath have so dashing an air,
> So charming a smirk, and agreeable stare,
> Not to say how they show all their shapes in the wind,
> With nothing before, and their pockets behind;
> Lac'd well at the head, and lac'd well at the foot,

Quite neat, and the boddice as tight as the boot,
Tho' the petticoat, once so important a charge,
Clings close to the limbs, or flies off all at large:
So, you know, 'twould be foolish to sweat and to pay
To see the long legs of the girls at the play,
You've the same sight for nothing just every day.
'Tis for this that a crony of mine takes his stand
At the door of the temple that's kept by Molland...
And there with his eyes, and a couple of glasses,
He views all the charms of each nymph as she passes:
Till at last all on fire at the sight of Miss S—
He quenches his flame in a basin of soup.

◆

Scoop, Sloop, Swoop? Whoever Miss S— was, she was doubtless practised in all kinds of feminine alchemy.

> BRING, O BRING thy essence-pot,
> Amber, musk, and bergamot,
> Eau de chipre, eau de luce,
> Sans pareil, and citron juice,
> Nor thy band-box leave behind,
> Fill'd with stores of every kind;
> All th' enraptur'd bard supposes,
> Who to Fancy odes composes;
> All that Fancy's self has feign'd,
> In a band-box is contained:
> Painted lawns, and chequer'd shades,
> Crape that's worn by love-lorn maids,

Water'd tabbies, flower'd brocades;
Vi'lets, pinks, Italian posies,
Myrtles, jessamins, and roses,
Aprons, caps, and 'kerchiefs clean,
Straw-built hats and bonnets green,
Catguts, gauzes, tippets, ruffs,
Fans, and hoods, and feather'd muffs,
Stomachers, and Paris-nets,
Ear-rings, necklaces, aigrets,
Fringes, blonds, and mignionets;
Fine vermillion for the cheek,
Velvet patches a la Grecque.
Come, but don't forget the gloves,
Which, with all the smiling loves,
Venus caught young Cupid picking
From the tender breast of chicken;
Little chicken, worthier far
Than the birds of Juno's car,
Soft as Cytherea's dove,
Let thy skin my skin improve;
Thou by night shall grace my arm,
And by day shall teach to charm.
Then, O sweet Goddess, bring with thee
Thy boon attendant Gaiety,
Laughter, Freedom, Mirth, and Ease,
And all the smiling deities;
Fancy spreading painted sails,
Loves that fan with gentle gales.
But hark! - methinks I hear a voice,

My organs all at once rejoice;
A voice that says, or seems to say,
"Sister, hasten, sister gay,
"Come to the pump-room – come away."

❖

That was Christopher Anstey, whose celebrated satire on the follies of Bath earnt him a niche in Poets' Corner in Westminster Abbey. He could spot a predatory widow.

BUT WHO is that bombasin lady so gay,
So profuse of her beauties in sable array;
How she rests on her heel, how she turns out her toe,
How she pulls down her stays, with her head up to shew
Her lily-white bosom that rivals the snow;
'Tis the widow Quicklackit, whose husband last week,
Poor Stephen, went suddenly forth in a pique,
And push'd off his boat for the Stygian creek:
Poor Stephen! he never return'd from the bourn,
But left the disconsolate widow to mourn:
Three times did she faint when she heard of the news;
Six days did she weep, and all comfort refuse;
But Stephen, no sorrows, no tears can recall;
So she hallows the seventh, and comes to the ball:

For some ladies at Bath, as for some gentlemen, the pursuit of a mate was a serious business. But for a couple of giggling teenagers, observed by Miss Austen, flirting was still a harmless game.

'FOR HEAVEN'S SAKE, let us move away from this end of the room. Do you know, there are two odious young men who have been staring at me this half-hour. They really put me quite out of countenance. Let us go and look at the arrivals. They will hardly follow us there.'

Away they walked to the book; and while Isabella examined the names, it was Catherine's employment to watch the proceedings of these alarming young men.

'They are not coming this way, are they? I hope they are not so impertinent as to follow us. Pray let me know if they are coming. I am determined I will not look up.'

In a few moments Catherine, with unaffected pleasure, assured her that she need not be longer uneasy, as the gentlemen had just left the Pump Room.

'And which way are they gone?' said Isabella, turning hastily round. 'One was a very good-looking young man.'

'They went towards the churchyard.'

'Well, I am amazingly glad I have got rid of them! And now, what say you to going to Edgar's Buildings with me, and looking at my new hat? You said you should like to see it.'

Catherine readily agreed. 'Only,' she added, 'perhaps we may overtake the two young men.'

'Oh, never mind that. If we make haste, we shall pass

Queen Street

by them presently, and I am dying to show you my hat.'

'But if we only wait a few minutes, there will be no danger of our seeing them at all.'

'I shall not pay them any such compliment, I assure you. I have no notion of treating men with such respect. That is the way to spoil them.'

Catherine had nothing to oppose against such reasoning; and therefore, to show the independence of Miss Thorpe, and her resolution of humbling the sex, they set off immediately as fast as they could walk, in pursuit of the two young men.

◆

Such adventures might begin innocuously enough, but where would they end? For Prudence Blunderhead, the naive heroine of Christopher Anstey's satire, the result seemed (to her) to have been a vision of Methodist bliss. Or — perish the thought — should we put a less spiritual, and more animal, interpretation on the sudden arrival of Roger the Methodist preacher in her room? Notice, incidentally, how Anstey celebrates the deflowering of Prudence with a parody of a Wesleyan hymn.

> BLESSED I, tho' once rejected,
>   Like a little wand'ring sheep,
> Who this morning was elected
>   By a vision in my sleep.

For I dream'd an apparition
    Came, like Roger, from above;
Saying, by divine commission,
    I must fill you full of love.

Just with Roger's head of hair on,
    Roger's mouth and pious smile;
Sweet, methinks, as beard of Aaron,
    Dropping down with holy oil.

I began to fall a-kicking,
    Panted, struggled, strove, in vain;
When the spirit whipt so quick in,
    I was cur'd of all my pain.

First I thought it was the night-mare
    Lay so heavy on my breast;
But I found new joy and light there,
    When with heav'nly love possest.

Come again then, apparition,
    Finish what thou has begun;
Roger, stay! thou soul's physician,
    I with thee my race will run.

❖

Not all poets treated affairs of the heart so flippantly. Those more susceptible to deep emotion, such as Thomas Hardy, might spend the night brooding about the unobtainable.

> ON BEECHEN CLIFF self-commune I
> This night of mid-June, mute and dry;
> When darkness never rises higher
> Than Bath's dim concave, towers, and spire,
> Last eveglow loitering in the sky
>
> To feel the dawn, close lurking by,
> The while the lamps as glow-worms lie
> In a glade, myself their lonely eyer
>   On Beechen Cliff:
>
> The city sleeps below. I sigh,
> For there dwells one, all testify,
> To match the maddest dream's desire:
> What swain with her would not aspire
> To walk the world, yea, sit but nigh
>   On Beechen Cliff!

◆

Bath itself was in sombre mood after the partying had ended and the visitors gone.

THE MUSIC and entertainments of Bath are over for this season; and all our gay birds of passage have taken their flight to Bristolwell, Tunbridge, Brighthelmstone, Scarborough, Harrowgate, &c. Not a soul is seen in this place, but a few broken-winded parsons, waddling like so many crows along the North Parade. There is always a great shew of the clergy at Bath: none of your thin, puny, yellow, hectic figures, exhausted with abstinence, and hard study, labouring under the *morbi eruditorum*, but great overgrown dignitaries and rectors, with rubicund noses and gouty ancles, or broad bloated faces, dragging along great swag bellies; the emblems of sloth and indigestion.

◆

Another aspect of Bath emerges, the place for rest and retirement. Here is a twentieth-century comment, by E.V. Lucas.

BATH may not be a bee, but she is a very beautiful drone. There is certainly no inland town in England with nothing to do that does it so gracefully and is so bland and dignified and comely. But when I say that Bath does nothing I mean only in comparison with what are called industrial towns, such as her neighbour Bristol. As a matter of fact, she does much, for in addition to having given us excellent biscuits since 1735, and since I know not when the sweet and sticky buns that are named after her, she cures the sick, strengthens the lame, and provides the most distinguished surroundings for those who prefer repose to activity: in fact, I can think of no more attractive haven in which to moor one's battered old hulk for the evening of life.

Bath is not only a drone herself, but makes drones of her guests, who in the business of idling can get through the day amusingly enough. I, personally, like to lean over the North Parade bridge, to watch the rapid Avon flowing below it and see the lovely Pulteney bridge, with its three perfect arches: a bridge which, when you are upon it, is not a bridge at all, but a section of a narrow street of shops.

◆

James Boswell took much the same view in 1776.

I WAS DELIGHTED with Bath. It was consolatory to see that there really is a place in the world to which one may retire, and be calm, placid and cheerful. Such is my notion of Bath, and I believe it is a general notion. Quin said it was the cradle of age, and a fine slope to the grave.

◆

Among the poets on that downward slope was Walter Savage Landor. In two sad poems he reflected on growing old in Bath.

ASKED TO DANCE AT BATH
In first position I can stand no longer;
A time there was when these two calves were stronger
And could move bravely up and down the Rooms,
But youthful days evaporate like perfumes.

TO BATH

The snows have fallen since my eyes were closed
      Upon thy downs and pine-woods, genial Bath!
In whose soft bosom my young head reposed,
      Whose willing hand shed flowers throughout
                                my path.
The snows have fallen on more heads than mine,
      Alas! on few with heavier cares opprest.
My early wreath of love didst thou entwine,
      Wilt thou entwine one for my last long rest?

❖

And when time ran out at last, there was one final accolade, the chance of immortality in marble. W.H. Hudson died in 1922 and his memorial, by Jacob Epstein, is in London, in Hyde Park. A few years earlier he had sat in Bath Abbey and pondered the matter.

I HAUNTED the abbey, and the more I saw of it the more I loved it. The impression it had made on me during my former visits had faded, or else I had never properly seen it, or had not seen it in the right emotional mood. Now I began to think it the best of all the great abbey churches of England and the equal of the cathedrals in its effect on the mind. How rich the interior is in its atmosphere of tempered light or tender gloom! How tall and graceful the columns holding up the high roof of white stone with its marvellous palm-leaf sculpture! What a vast expanse of beautifully stained glass! I certainly gave myself plenty of time to appreciate it on this occasion, as I visited it every day, sometimes two or three times, and not infrequently I sat there for an hour at a stretch.

Sitting there one day, thinking of nothing, I was gradually awakened to a feeling almost of astonishment at the sight of the extraordinary number of memorial tablets of every imaginable shape and size which crowd the walls. So numerous are they and so closely placed that you could not find space anywhere to put your hand against the wall. We are accustomed to think that in cathedrals and other great ecclesiastical buildings the illustrious dead receive burial, and their names and claims on our gratitude and reverence are recorded, but in no fane in the land is there so numerous a gathering of the dead as in this place. The inscription-covered walls were like the pages of an old black-letter volume without margins. Yet when I came to think of it I could not recall any Bath celebrity or great person associated with Bath except Beau Nash, who was not perhaps a very great person. Probably Carlyle would have described him as a 'meeserable creature'.

Leaving my seat I began to examine the inscriptions, and found that they had not been placed there in memory of men belonging to Bath or even Somerset. These monuments were erected to persons from all counties in the three kingdoms, and from all the big towns, those to

Londoners being most numerous. Nor were they of persons distinguished in any way. Here you find John or Henry or Thomas Smith, or Brown, or Jones, or Robinson, provision dealer, or merchant, of Clerkenwell, or Bermondsey, or Bishopsgate Street Within or Without; also many retired captains, majors, and colonels. There were hundreds more whose professions or occupations in life were not stated. There were also hundreds of memorials to ladies - widows and spinsters. They were all, in fact, to persons who had come to die in Bath after 'taking the waters', and dying, they or their friends had purchased immortality on the walls of the abbey with a handful or two of gold.

◆

There is a kind of awful paradox here, as the guidebook current in Hudson's day was at pains to point out.

AS A REMINDER of Bath's once fashionable days, the walls of the aisles are covered with memorials of local celebrities; amongst them there is a tablet to Nash. The tomb of Lady Waller, and Garrick's epitaph on Quin should perhaps also be noticed. As Dr. Harington's sprightly epigram suggests, this portentous display of mortality is not an inspiring study for visitors who come to Bath to take "the cure".

> These walls, adorned with monument and bust,
> Show how Bath waters serve to lay the dust.

Pulteney Bridge

Bath's message seems to be that millennia have not changed human aspirations. Ordinary Roman worshippers at Minerva's temple felt just the same.

THIS holy spot, wrecked by insolent hands and cleansed afresh, Gaius Severius Emeritus, centurion in charge of the region, has restored to the Virtue and Deity of the Emperor.

TO THE SPIRITS of the departed: Gaius Calpurnius Receptus, priest of the goddess Sulis, lived seventy-five years. Calpurnia Trifosa, his freedwoman and wife, had this set up.

LUCIUS Vitellius Tancinus, son of Mantaius, a tribesman of Caurium in Spain, trooper of the cavalry regiment of Vettones, Roman citizens, aged forty-six, of twenty-six years' service, lies buried here.

TO THE SPIRITS of the departed and to Successa Petronia, who lived three years, four months, nine days, Vettius Romulus and Victoria Sabina set this up to their dearest daughter.

◆

Perhaps, mused Hardy, the deities of the pagan temple and the Christian abbey should proclaim a truce.

THE CHIMES called midnight, just at interlune,
And the daytime parle on the Roman investigations
Was shut to silence, save for the husky tune
The bubbling waters played near the excavations.

And a warm air came up from underground,
And the flutter of a filmy shape unsepulchred,
That collected itself, and waited, and looked around:
Nothing was seen, but utterances could be heard:

Those of the Goddess whose shrine was beneath the pile
Of the God with the baldachined altar overhead:
'And what did you win by raising this nave and aisle
Close on the site of the temple I tenanted?

The notes of your organ have thrilled down out of view
To the earth-clogged wrecks of my edifice many a year,
Though stately and shining once - ay, long ere you
Had set up crucifix and candle here.

Your priests have trampled the dust of mine without rueing,
Despising the joys of man whom I so much loved,
Though my springs boil on by your Gothic arcades and pewing,
And sculptures crude... Would Jove they could be removed!'

'Repress, O lady proud, your traditional ires;
You know not by what a frail thread we equally hang;
It is said we are images both - twitched by people's desires;
And that I, as you, fail like a song men yesterday sang!'

'What – a Jumping-jack you, and myself but a poor Jumping-jill,
Now worm-eaten, times agone twitched at Humanity's bid?
O I cannot endure it! - But, chance to us whatso there will,
Let us kiss and be friends! Come, agree you?' - None heard if he did...

And the olden dark hid the cavities late laid bare,
And all was suspended and soundless as before,
Except for a gossamery noise fading off in the air,
And the boiling voice of the waters' medicinal pour.

Thomas Hardy, so sensitive to the atmosphere of place, had picked up a feeling about Bath - the juxtaposition of old and new, grand and decayed - which other writers too have sensed. An anonymous Anglo-Saxon poet observed the ruins of Bath, and mused on the transience of cities.

> STRANGE to behold is the masonry
> Broken by fate.
> The city is fractured,
> The giants' fortress decaying,
> The roofs are fallen,
> The towers tottering,
> Wooden gate roofless,
> Rime on the mortar,
> Shattered shelters,
> Time-scarred, tempest-marred,
> Undermined by age.
> Earth's grasp holds
> Its mighty builders
> Tumbled, crumbled
> In gravel's hard grip;

As a hundred generations
Of men pass away.
Lichen-spotted grey and orange,
This wall often witnessed
One great man after another,
As it withstood the storms...
Bright were the buildings,
Bathing halls many,
Lofty gables in profusion,
War-clang frequent,
Mead-halls many,
Merriment frequenting;
Till all was overwhelmed
By fate the unrelenting.
Breaches broke the walls,
Baleful days came on,
Death swept off
The valiant men.
Their armouries became
Razed to their foundations;
The city crumbled away.
Rebuilders, overcome,
Lay dead upon the earth.
And so these halls are dreary rubble,
And the crimson curving
Tiles are tumbling
From the encircling frame of rafters:
The falling on the fallen,
Debris heaved in heaps;

Where many a warrior once
In splendour attired,
Proud and flushed with wine,
Shining in his armour;
Looked on silver treasures,
Intricate jewels,
And wealth and stores
And precious stones;
And on this bright city
Of broad dominion.
There stood a hall of stone;
The stream hotly issued
With eddies widening
Up to the wall encircling all
The bright-bosomed pool.
There the baths
Arranged for use
Were hot with inward heat.

Royal Crescent

And even the fops and beaux of Regency Bath, men such as Cam Hobhouse, could be swayed by the thought that the good things of life do not last for ever. One day their Bath, and our Bath, will be a memory.

BUT, ALAS! what can Time the destroyer withstand?
Where's Troy? where's the May-pole, that rose in the Strand?
E'en thou, noble city! must perish, and if
Beacon Hill shall shake hands with his friend Beachen Cliff,
(As a prophet foretold, and fixing the day,
Drove all true believers in terror away,)
Then with no slow-consumption, but swallow'd entire,
Thy mirth and thy music at once shall expire.
All at once shall be crush'd both the old and the young
Of all who so caper'd, and all who so sung,
Of Square, Crescent, Circus, no traces remain,
And the valley of Bladud be turn'd to a plain.
Yet still on that plain the green surface shall show
Some signs of the Wonders once working below;
For still shall thy streams of hot water be found,
Still the caverns return no unmusical sound;
And the shepherd shall swear, whilst attending his flock,
That he hears us a footing it under the rock.

❖

Sources and Acknowledgements ~

The compiler wishes to express his gratitude to the staff of Bath Reference Library, University of Bristol Library, and Trowbridge Local Studies Library, for affording research facilities; and to the copyright owners individually acknowledged below for permitting quotation from copyright items.

9: Tobias Smollett, *The expedition of Humphry Clinker*, 1771
10-11: Samuel Pepys, *The diary of Samuel Pepys* (12th-14th June 1668)
11: Christopher Morris, *The journeys of Celia Fiennes*, 1949
12: William Stukeley, *Itinerarium curiosum*, 2nd ed., 1776
13: Francis Kilvert, *Kilvert's diary*, 3 vols. (ed. William Plomer), 1938-40
14: W.H. Hudson, *Birds and man*, 1915
15-16: W.H. Hudson, *Afoot in England*, 1909
16: J.B. Priestley, *English Journey*, 1933
16-17: Jane Austen, *Persuasion*, 1818
17-18: Horace Walpole, *Horace Walpole's correspondence* (ed. W.S. Lewis, vols. 10 and 31: letters of 5th-6th October 1766)
19: Daniel Defoe, *A tour thro' the whole island of Great Britain*, 3rd ed. (ed. Samuel Richardson), 1742, vol.2
19: Gaius Julius Solinus, *Collectanea rerum memorabilium*, 3rd century
20-1: John Higgins, *The firste parte of the mirour for magistrates*, 1610 ed.
22: John Rastell, *The pastyme of people*, 1529
23: Thomas Fuller, *The worthies of England*, 1662
24-5: Daniel Defoe, *A tour thro' the whole island of Great Britain*, 3rd ed. (ed. Samuel Richardson), 1742, vol.2
26: William Stukeley, *Itinerarium curiosum*, 2nd ed., 1776
26-7: Charles Dickens, *The Pickwick Papers*, 1837
27-9: Tobias Smollett, *An essay on the external use of water*, 1752
30-1: Tobias Smollett, *The expedition of Humphry Clinker*, 1771
31-2: John Cam Hobhouse, *Wonders of a week at Bath*, 1811
32-4: Thomas Guidott, *The register of Bath; or two hundred observations containing an account of cures...*, 2nd ed., 1724
35: Charles Dickens, *The Pickwick Papers*, 1837
35: Daniel Defoe, *A tour thro' the whole island of Great Britain*, 1st ed., 1724-7

36: Tobias Smollett, *The expedition of Humphry Clinker*, 1771

37: R.S.O. Tomlin, 'The curse tablets', in Barry Cunliffe (ed.), *The temple of Sulis Minerva at Bath*, vol.2, 1988 (with the author's permission)

38: Charles Dickens, *The Pickwick Papers*, 1837

38-9: Tobias Smollett, *The expedition of Humphry Clinker*, 1771

39-40: Jane Austen, *Persuasion*, 1818

40-1: Oliver Goldsmith, *The life of Richard Nash, Esq., late Master of the Ceremonies at Bath...*, 1762

41-2: Christopher Morris, *The journeys of Celia Fiennes*, 1949

43-4: Daniel Defoe, *A tour thro' the whole island of Great Britain*, 3rd ed. (ed. Samuel Richardson), 1742, vol.2

45-6: Mary Chandler, *The description of Bath: a poem...*, 8th ed., 1767

46: Daniel Defoe, *A tour thro' the whole island of Great Britain*, 3rd ed. (ed. Samuel Richardson), 1742, vol.2

47-8: Joyce Hemlow (ed.), *The journals and letters of Fanny Burney (Madame d'Arblay)*, vol.1, 1972

50-2: Oliver Goldsmith, *The life of Richard Nash, Esq., late Master of the Ceremonies at Bath...*, 1762

53: Charles Dickens, *The Pickwick Papers*, 1837

53-5: Geoffrey Chaucer, *The Canterbury tales*, c.1390 (The Wife of Bath's tale)

55-6: Daniel Defoe, *Moll Flanders*, 1722

56-7: John Cam Hobhouse, *Wonders of a week at Bath*, 1811

57-9: Christopher Anstey, *The new Bath guide*, 1766

60-2: Jane Austen, *Northanger Abbey*, 1818

62-3: Christopher Anstey, *The new Bath guide*, 1766

64: Thomas Hardy, *Human shows, far phantasies, songs and trifles*, 1925

64-5: Tobias Smollett, *The expedition of Humphry Clinker*, 1771

65-6: E.V. Lucas, *English leaves*, 1933

66: C.B. Tinker (ed.), *The letters of James Boswell*, vol.1, 1925

66-7: Walter Savage Landor, *The complete works...* (ed. Stephen Wheeler), vol.16, 1936

67-9: W.H. Hudson, *Afoot in England*, 1909

69: G.W. and J.H. Wade, *Somerset*, 6th ed., 1923 (The Little Guides)

70-1: cited in Barry Cunliffe, *Roman Bath*, 1969 (with author's permission)

71-2: Thomas Hardy, *Satires of circumstance, lyrics and reveries*, 1914

73-5: adapted from text in R.F. Leslie, *Three old English elegies*, 1961, and translation by J. Earle in *Proceedings of the Bath Natural History and Antiquarian Field Club*, vol.2, 1871

76: John Cam Hobhouse, *Wonders of a week at Bath*, 1811

A Miscellany of Explanations ~

Beacon Hill: high ground north of Bath, overlooking the London Road and Bathwick areas
Beechen Cliff: high ground south of the railway station, commanding fine views over the city
Bloody Buildings: Bladud Buildings, southern end of The Paragon
boxtone: Buxton, Derbyshire
Brightelmstone: former name for Brighton
Bristolwell: presumably Hotwells, Bristol
chyle: digested food converted to fluid in the stomach and intestine prior to absorption
Clarton: Claverton (Down), high ground south-east of Bath
cowitch: cowage, a stinging plant which causes itching
Crashit: Crescent, i.e. The Royal Crescent
Harry King's Row: Harlequin Row, i.e Vineyards, the Huntingdon Chapel area
Hottogon: The Octagon, off Milsom Street
Johnson Street: now Johnstone Street
julep: medicated drink sweetened with syrup or sugar
killibeate: chalybeate, mineral water containing iron
Laura Place: the western end of Great Pulteney Street
lewis-holes: holes made for gripping stone between the jaws of a lewis, a type of crane
Milsham-street: now Milsom Street
Molland: a pastry-cook whose shop was in Milsom Street, c.1810
morbi eruditorum: illnesses brought on by too much studying
nigromancyer: necromancer, a kind of magician
Quin: James Quin, famous Irish actor, died at Bath 1766
Stygian creek: River Styx, across which in Classical mythology dead souls were ferried

Index ~

abbey 10-14, 16, 30, 42, 49, 67-9, 72-3
Allen, Ralph 24, 44-6, 50
Anstey, Christopher 57-60, 62-3
Austen, Jane 16-17, 39-40, 60, 62
Avon, River 14-15, 18, 44-5, 66
balls 18, 32, 38, 50-2, 59
Barrow Hill 14
bathing 9-10, 19, 27-9, 35
Beacon Hill 76, 79
Beechen Cliff 64, 76, 79
Bennet, Matthew 32-3
Bladud 20-2, 76
Bladud Buildings 9, 79
Boswell, James 66
Brookes, Thomas 33-4
building operations 46-8
Burney, Fanny 47-8
Camden Crescent 15
Camden Place 16
Carlyle, Thomas 68
chairs, sedan 10, 29, 42, 52
Chandler, Mary 45-6
Chatham, Lord 18
Chaucer, Geoffrey 53-5
chyle 25, 34, 79
Circus 9, 15, 31
Claverton Down 24, 79
clergymen 65
complaints and illnesses 20-1, 23, 25-6, 31-4
cosmetics 57-8
costume 58
courtship and flirting 53-7, 59-60, 62-3
cures 32-4
death 28-9, 31-2, 66-71
Defoe, Daniel 35, 43-4, 55-6
Dickens, Charles 26-7, 35, 38, 53
dishonesty 36-7
doctors 28, 30-2
Edgar's Buildings 60
epitaphs 68-71
Fiennes, Celia 11, 41-2
flirting and courtship 53-7, 59-60, 62-3
Fuller, Thomas 23
Goldsmith, Oliver 40-1, 50-2
Guidott, Thomas 32-4
Guildhall 38
Hardy, Thomas 64, 71-3
Harington, Dr 69
Harlequin Row 9, 79
Higgins, John 20-1
Hobhouse, Cam 31-2, 56-7, 76
How, James 34
Hudson, W.H. 14-16, 67-9
illnesses and complaints 20-1, 23, 25-6, 31-4
Johnstone Street 48, 79
Kilvert, Francis 13
Kingsmead 41-2
Landor, W.S. 66-7
Lansdown 24
Lansdown Road 29
Laura Place 40, 48, 79
lodgings 11, 29, 41-2, 46
Lucas, E.V. 65-6
Methodism 62-3
Milsom Street 31, 79
Molland 57, 79
Nash, Richard 'Beau' 41, 50-2, 68-9
North Parade 65, 66
Octagon 9, 79
Pepys, Samuel 10-11
Priestley, J.B. 16
Pulteney Bridge 43, 66, 70
Pump Room 12, 16, 18, 26, 28, 30, 47-8, 59-60; *see also* rooms
Queen Street 61
Quiet Street 8, 15
Quin, James 66, 69, 79
Rastell, John 22
retirement 65
Richardson, Samuel 19, 24-5, 43-4, 46
Romans 19, 37, 43, 70-2
rooms 17, 39, 41, 66; *see also* Pump Room
Royal Crescent 9, 75, 79
Ruin, The 73-5
servants 9, 26-7, 36, 43
Sion Hill 15
Smollett, Tobias 9, 27-31, 36, 38-9, 64-5
snobbery 39-40
Solinus 19
Spring Gardens 48
stone 14, 43-6
Stukeley, William 12, 26
Vane, Lady 18
walls, town 10, 43
Walpole, Horace 17-18
waters 20, 23-7, 30-1, 35, 72, 76
Wood, John 50